My Farm

My Sheep

By Heather Miller

Children's Press
A Division of Grolier Publishing
New York / London / Hong Kong / Sydney
Danbury, Connecticut

Photo Credits: Cover, pp. 5, 7, 9, 11, 13, 15, 17, 21 by Thaddeus Harden; p. 19 © Index Stock Imagery

Contributing Editor: Jennifer Ceaser
Book Design: MaryJane Wojciechowski

Visit Children's Press on the Internet at:
http://publishing.grolier.com

Library of Congress Cataloging-in-Publication Data

Miller, Heather.
   My sheep / by Heather Miller.
      p. cm. — (My farm)
   Includes bibliographical references and index.
   Summary: A young girl describes how she cares for the sheep living on her farm.
   ISBN 0-516-23110-3 (lib. bdg.) — ISBN 0-516-23035-2 (pbk.)
   1. Sheep—Juvenile literature. [1. Sheep.] I. Title.

 SF375.2.M53 2000
 636.3—dc21

                                                            00-024363

Contents

My name is Audrey.

Welcome to my sheep farm!

This is Belle.

Belle is a **ewe**.

A ewe is a mother sheep.

This is Belle's **lamb**.

A lamb is a baby sheep.

9

A lamb can always find its mother.

The lamb just has to listen for her special **bleat**.

A bleat sounds like this: "Baaaaaaa!"

I feed my sheep **grain**.

They eat the grain from a **trough**.

13

My sheep grow coats in the winter.

Their coats are called **fleece**.

Fleece keeps the sheep warm when it is cold.

15

In the spring, Dad shaves off the fleece.

It doesn't hurt the sheep.

It's like giving the sheep a haircut!

The fleece is made of **wool**.

The wool is used to make **yarn**.

At night, my sheep go to sleep in a **pen**.

The straw on the floor keeps them warm.

Goodnight, my sheep!

New Words

bleat **(bleet)** the sound a sheep makes

ewe **(yu)** a mother sheep

fleece **(flees)** a sheep's coat

grain **(grayn)** food that sheep eat

lamb **(lam)** a baby sheep

pen **(pen)** a place where sheep are kept

trough **(trof)** something that holds food for farm animals

wool **(wul)** what a sheep's coat is made of

yarn **(yarn)** thick thread made from wool

To Find Out More

Books

Hooray For Sheep Farming
by Bobbie Kalman
Crabtree

Sheep
by Peter Brady
Capstone Books

Web Sites

Barnyard Buddies
http://www.execpc.com/~byb/
Meet the Barnyard Buddies and learn more about farm animals.
Play animal games and send an e-mail to your favorite animal!

Sounds of the World's Animals—Sheep
http://www.georgetown.edu/cball/animals/sheep.html
Click on a sheep's picture and listen to it bleat!

Index

About the Author

Heather Miller lives in Cambridge, Massachusetts, with her son, Jasper. She is a graduate student at Harvard University.

Reading Consultants

Kris Flynn, Coordinator, Small School District Literacy, The San Diego County Office of Education

Shelly Forys, Certified Reading Recovery Specialist, W.J. Zahnow Elementary School, Waterloo, IL

Peggy McNamara, Professor, Bank Street College of Education, Reading and Literacy Program